MW01702199

Hot Tub Etiquette

The official behavioral conduct and complete guide for hot tubs

The secret language of the tub, communication, hacks, tips and tricks, do's and don'ts, interesting facts, and first hand experience.

Full checklist for your perfect hot tub experience inside

Field Researcher

Nathaniel Cheddar- Hot Tub and Spa expert

Contents

Introduction

Everyone enjoys going to the pool but sometimes people decide they want to take it to the next step and relax in the hot tub. This is your guide to that next step.

Chapter 1: Conditions

In this chapter

Appropriate timing
Weather/seasons
Proper Spas
Day and Night

If you are in the mood or are predicting you will soon be in the mood to go to the hot tub there are some things you need to take into account. The last thing you want for yourself and your party is to encounter another party. Lucky for you, you own the "Hot tub etiquette" book! Let's dive in and see how you can take your experience to the next level!

Timing

Timing is key when it comes to enjoying a delightful hot tub experience. This calendar allows you to see the estimated hot tub population

	Jan	Feb	Mar	Apr	May	Jun	Jul	Aug	Sep	Oct	Nov	Dec
AM	8-11	8-11	8-11	8-11	8-11	8-11	8-11	8-11	8-11	8-11	8-11	8-11
PM	12-6	12-6	12-6	12-6	12-6	12-6 X	12-6 X	12-6 X	12-6	12-6	12-6	12-6
PM	7-11	7-11	7-11 X	7-11 X	7-11 X	7-11 X	7-11 X	7-11 X	7-11	7-11	7-11	7-11

X: High Risk

The hot tub becomes a favored excursion during the summertime. Recreational members of the hot tub community dislike this time of the year. This specific time of the year adds a lot of variables to the table.

Summer vs Winter

Summer is the worst when it comes to finding an uninhabited jacuzzi. Hot tubs will be full by the dozens across one's city. Unlike summer, winter is the best time to embark in a hot tub session. Children will typically be attending school, Casual and recreational users will stick to their time charts, and last but not least, it will be not as hot out leading into longer excursions.

Winter Benefits-

Although winter is cooler, it is the preferred hot tub condition. The population is typically low during winter. Here is a list of Wintertime Benefits-

-Longer acclimation

-Low populations

-Cleanliness enhancement

-and many more!

Winter Disadvantages-

By now you now see that winter is the prime time to relax in the hot tub undisturbed. It isn't all perfect in the winter hot tub world. Here are some down sides-

-Longer reverse acclimation

-Frequent Rainy Day schedule

-Unexpected heat shut offs

-Non heated hot tubs

Sure thing! Hot tubs during the wintertime might not be heated. What this means for you and your party-

-Hot tub fallback charts (Located in the back of the book)

Check your fallback charts for other local hot tubs that may be heated

Finding the right hot tub

Finding the perfect hot tub for you and your party can be difficult at times. Even after finding a vacant hot tub that is heated, there are a few more variables that may impact your experience. These are the questions you should ask before you commit to a submersion.

Is the water clear or cloudy?

Murky waters means many things for yourself and your party. Doing a full body submersion in murky waters can result in rashes, infections, and irritations. As long as you take a shower after the session, you will most likely be just fine!

Reasons for the murky water or the musty smells-

-Has not been cleaned
-On site sex has took stage prior
-Soap prank product

Take account of these scenarios and ask yourself *is it worth it?*

Do the spa jets work? And if not, have you tried pushing the emergency shut off switch?

The jets aren't for everyone but for the members of your party that do prefer them.

Bonus questions that might not be necessary include-

How big is the tub?
How is the wind blowing today?

Day opposed to Night

Night Time hot tub adventures tend to present us with remarkable memories in opposition to Day Time sessions. Day Time sessions don't feel as lively and they aren't preferred. Reasons to go during the day would include-

-Being a parental
-Not having time to go to the spa during night hours
-Scared of teenagers
-Summer fun

Day Time hot tubbers tend to either be children or parents. Typically it's never anything in between. You may be asking yourself, why parents specifically? That is because an adult is not the same as a parental.

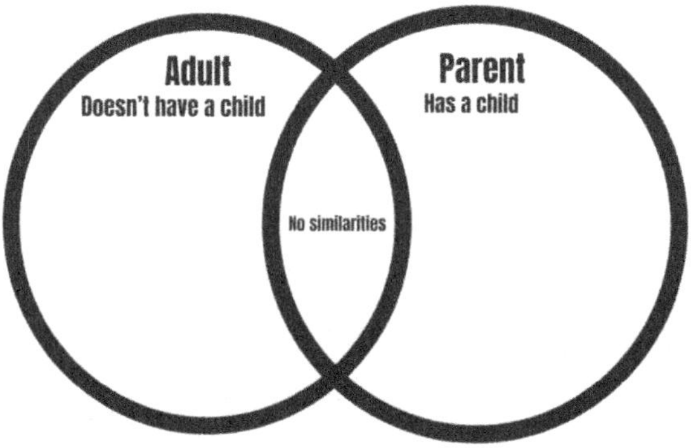

Parents have their reasons for coming to the hot tub during daylight hours. Research leads us to believe that their children are responsible for this.

If you meet any of those specifications within the Day Time hot tub checklist, then the best option would be to visit the hot tub during daylight hours.

Chapter 2: Approach

In this chapter

Signs

Tactics

Methods

By now you have a basic understanding of your preferred hot tub time and when it is acceptable to have a pleasant experience. One key concept when it comes to the hot tub community is, *approach.*

Hot tub signage

As we all know, the hot tub is available to people who reside locally to select hot tubs. If you aren't checking your charts or if you get unlucky you might have an encounter.

To prevent an encounter you can read these several signs to help you get the most of your hot tub experience.

Step One: Arrival

Upon arrival of said hot tub, thou should scan the area for vehicle transports. This isn't as easy as it may seem. This is your typical neighborhood, people park their cars next to their homes. This is how to tell whether the vehicle belongs to a resident or a rival hot tubber.

The vehicle in this image presents itself closer to the home opposed to the *pool area.* In most cases this means that this person is not attending the hot tub.

The vehicle in this image shows a car parked fairly close to the pool area. In many cases this would mean the hot tub is more than likely not vacant. If you are not sure then you will now need to approach step number two.

Step Two: Listen

Upon completing step number one, you must park your vehicular. Once you finish that you will need to either roll a window down or perhaps even get out of the vehicle.

The main goal for step number two is to listen for chatter, splashing or spa jets. In most cases these three sounds means the hot tub is in use.

Chattering and splashing means there is a 100 percent chance the spa is in use. The jets on the other hand is a different story.

Our research team found that people tend to set the jets for an extended amount of time. The hot tub members might not stay for the jet's full cycle. In this case if you only hear jets and none of the other two noises you will need to engage in step three.

Step Three: Peek

Step three can be quite difficult for the average spa goer, as you need to escape from your personal comfort zone. As you journey your way over to the surrounding fence. You must find a *peek hole*. Peek holes are typically small gaps or narrow slits where one's eye can examine the hot tub for rival tub goers.

The goal of using the peek hole method is to allow you to view within the hot tub's premises while your person remains hidden. By the end of this step you will know whether the hot tub has people in it or not.

Approach types-

Diving deeper into step three, there are two different approaches. The *silent approach* and the *loud and proud approach.*

To plan out what approach you should take, you need to count your party. If you finish counting and wind up with three or less, you should stick to the less obvious silent approach. If you are counting up your party and notice you have five or more, then the loud and proud approach would be the better option.

If you are wondering why a loud and proud approach would ever be better than the silent approach here is the list of benefits.

Benefits to 5+ party(Loud and Proud Approach)
-possible overthrow of hot tub vacancy
-fear the other tub goers into fleeing the tub early

The Loud and Proud Approach-
All five or more party members begin walking towards the pool area talking confidently and loud. As the party approaches the pool area you will begin to notice *absolute silence.* Absolute silence will grant you control over what happens next. You can either scan using the peek method or just barge on in.

Choosing the peek method, would entitle you and your party to reside in the pool/pool area for the remaining duration of the other party's hot tub session.

Choosing the barge method would allow your group to join the rival party's session. This method is viewed as disrespectful in the hot tub community but if done correctly you can have a pleasant hot tub experience. Barging can ensure that the opponent's party will leave soon and grant your party more time in your session.
One issue with the barge method is the possibility of an *awkward situation.* This situation may be encountered if you

utilize the barge method and the rival party outnumbers your party. In this case, you must reside in the pool area until the opponent's party finishes their affair.

Chapter 3: Communication

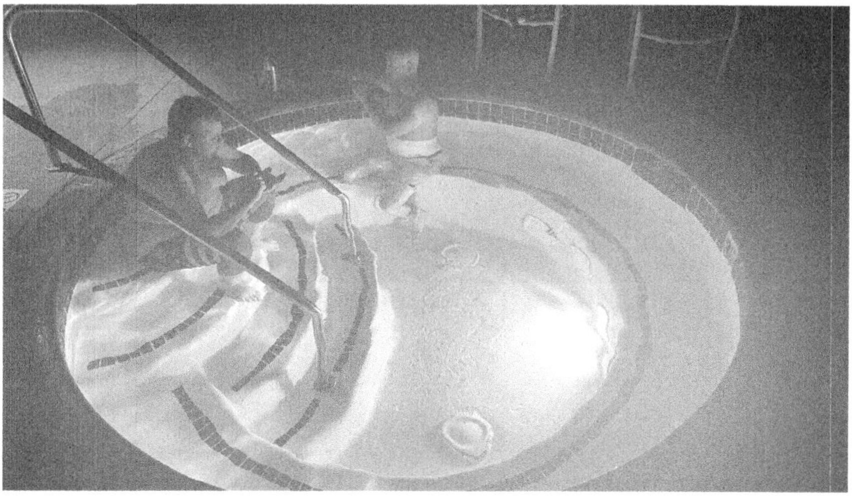

In this chapter

Body language

Dominance

Engagement

Small Talk

-Temperature
-Jets(on/off)

Any other forms of small talk will not get either party and or members far. Engagement isn't necessary in the hot tub because it is a place to reside. No one really wants small talk. Small talk is just about the worst conversation piece when it comes to the hot tub, so avoid it.

Conversation(Night)

Seeing distant acquaintances can make an awkward situation within the hot tub. In most cases it is best to not acknowledge them and pretend you don't know them. The members are here for the same reason, no conversations need to be exchanged.

Exchanging conversation to a close acquaintance is always good only if they are close enough. Not exchanging conversation with these types of acquaintances will lead to off site awkwardness. Conversation starters for these types of acquaintances would be common talk you would regularly have with them.

There are exceptions for common talk. Times you should not engage in conversation with them would be if there are female members. It doesn't matter how many there are. Never engage in conversation with a close acquaintance accompanied by a female.

The second you hear the loud and proud method, you will need to do these steps-

-Talk louder than the party outside of the spa
-Splash the water here and there(sounds like there are more people)
- Do not stop communication with the members of your party

Using these rebuttal tactics will grant success nearly every single time. If your party is able to assert dominance over other parties, then you will have the hot tub to yourselves. The loud and Proud combination with the barge in method will not work if the other party is louder.

It is all about dominance when it comes to the hot tub.

Small Talk

Communication within the hot tub can be extremely awkward if you aim conversation to the wrong person. Attempting small talk to someone who does not want to be provoked can backfire, making it more awkward for everyone.

Small talk is typically only acceptable if a member within a party knows a member from another party. Small talk outside of this situation will only allow for more awkward situations.

Small talk does not include saying "Hi" or "Bye". The only acceptable forms of small talk would be talk that involves the hot tub itself. Options would include-

The members in absolute silence facing in an odd direction wish to flee the hot tub but can't get the courage to leave. Typically this happens when a party uses the loud and proud technique with the barge in method and outnumbers the member. This member is forced to remain in the hot tub so they don't look like they are leaving because of the new party. Usually this member will remain in the hot tub five to ten minutes prior to the new party that entered. This instance and situation is formally known as the *last straggler*. These last stragglers will feel obligated to leave the spa but won't so they can assert whatever dominance they have left.

Dominance

Asserting dominance is essential when going to the spa. The party's with the most dominance will entitle them to respect and comfortable space within the pool area. There are many ways to assert dominance even before entering the hot tub.

-Playing loud music
-Slamming vehicle doors
-Revving engine

These tactics ensure you and party to a pleasant hot tub experience. Asserting dominance early on will nearly guarantee your capability of entering the spa.

If roles are reversed and you and your party are in the spa and you hear these tactics, you will need to act quickly. Typical tub goers will go silent and lose every ounce of dominance resulting in absolute silence. Avoid absolute silence at all costs if you are in the hot tub.

Communication is resented in the hot tub community. There are rare occasions where communication is necessary. To know when these occasions are, first we need to check out body language and the secret language within the hot tub.

Assuming you took the loud and proud approach along with the barge in method you now must be wondering what to do with yourself now. Being in a hot tub with strangers can be awkward. Absolute silence is common in a hot tub with two separate parties. Detecting body language is the ideal tactic here.

Body Language

Examining the other members of the hot tub is essential for reading body language. If the opposing members are faced away from the center of the tub, then it is a no go for any form of communication. Typically these hostile tub members are unfriendly and do not wish to partake in any form of engagement.

People on their phones means they are swing speakers, as they often are okay with either. They are typically the simplest of the hot tub profiling charts.

The members in silence facing the center of the hot tub mean they want to engage within a conversation. These members typically come to the hot tub for socializing purposes. It is often better to not socialize with these ones as it may distract you from your own hot tub experience.

Conversation (Day)

Holding up a conversation in the hot tub is one of the most brutal things a person will ever have to do in their lives. During the day you perhaps might find it slightly easier. Whenever you attend the hot tub during the day, you are going knowing there are possibilities that there will be someone there. If you check out our charts you will see the early hours throughout the year will tend to have less people in the hot tubs. The issue here is that when you go to the spa at night, your worst possible nightmare is an encounter. During the day an encounter isn't as bad. Here are benefits to possible conversations-

-Visibility levels high
-Lower dominance levels
-typically adults(not parents)

With these benefits here it will be a lot easier to engage in a conversation. In most situations, talking to other parties during the daylight is encouraged. Sitting in absolute silence is the worst during the day, as you can see everyone in clear visibility. Awkward situations tend to arise during the day if absolute silence is achieved.

Chapter 4: Profiling

In this chapter

Tub Members
How to Tell
Expectations
Vehicles
Neighborhood Exploration

Day and Night have two separate ways of handling conversations. Distinct people attend these different hot tub hours. So it is key to know which type of person you are in the hot tub with or about to be in the hot tub with.

Knowing the different members of the hot tub can take your hot tub experience to the next level.

The Elder-

Two Variants-

-Male

-Female

Typically seen in

-Dec from 7am-11am

-Jan from 8am-12pm

-March from 10am-1pm

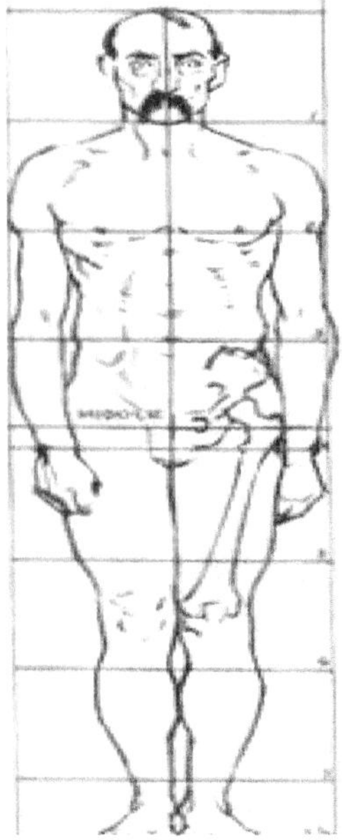

Key signs:

-White hair

-Slowed submersion and ascendance

-Shorter than adult

The Female-

Typically seen in

-June from 12pm-8pm

-July from 12pm-9-pm

-August-12pm-7pm

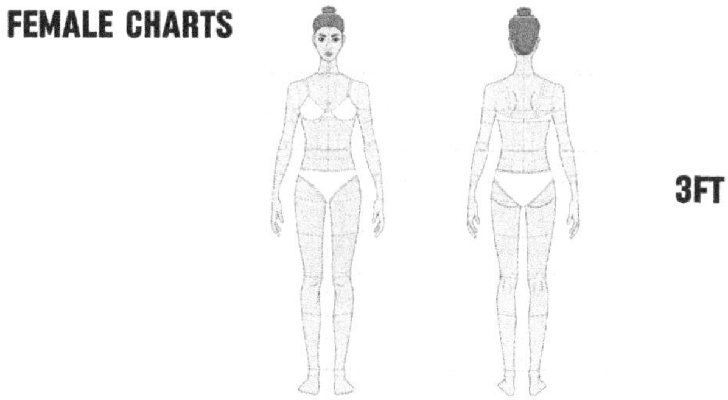

Key Signs:

-Longer hair

-Bikini swim gear

-Utilizing cellular device

The Male-

Typically seen in

-Jun from 6pm-8pm

-July from 6pm-8pm

-August from 6pm-8pm

MALE CHARTS

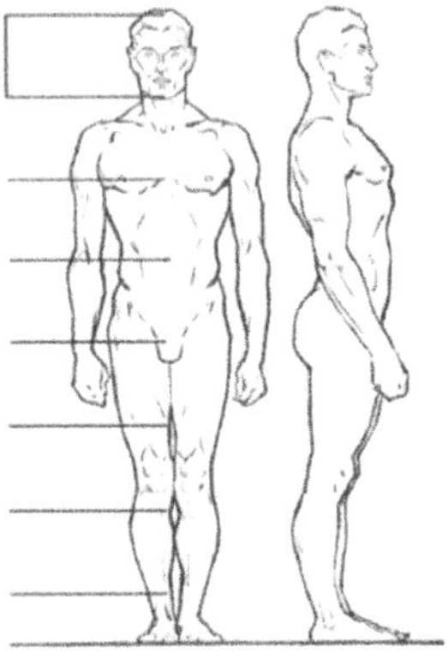

Key Signs:

-Shorter hair

-*Trunks*

-Seen in parties of 2+

-Never alone

The Adult-

Two Variants-

-Male

-Female

Typically seen in

-Jun from 5pm-9pm

-July from 6pm-9pm

-August from 5pm-8pm

ADULT CHARTS

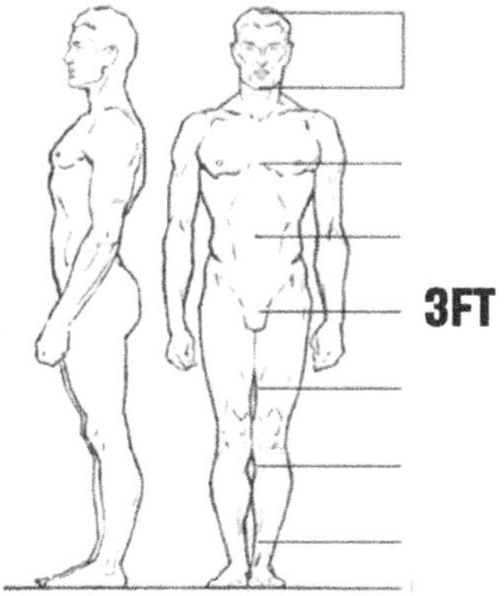

Key Signs:

-Not accompanied by child

-More dominant than parent

-Seen frequently in *after hours*

-Seen in parties of 2+

The Parent-

Two Variants-

-Male

-Female

Typically seen in

-March from 6pm-7pm

-May from 5pm-7pm

-Jun from 1pm-8pm

-July from 12pm-9pm

-August from 11am-8pm

The Child-

Typically seen in

-May from 5pm-6pm

-Jun from 1pm-6pm

-July from 12pm-5pm

-August from 11am-3pm

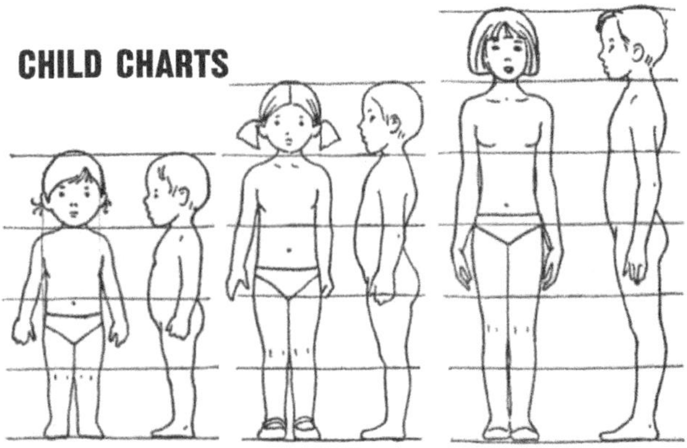

Key Signs:

Smaller

-High pitch voice

-Splashing

-Staring problems

-Accompanied by parental

The Teen-

Typically seen in

-March from 7pm-9pm

-April from 7pm-9pm

-May from 7pm-9pm

-Jun from 8pm-10pm

-July from 8pm-11pm

-August from 7pm-9pm

ADULT, TEEN, CHILD, COMPARISON CHART

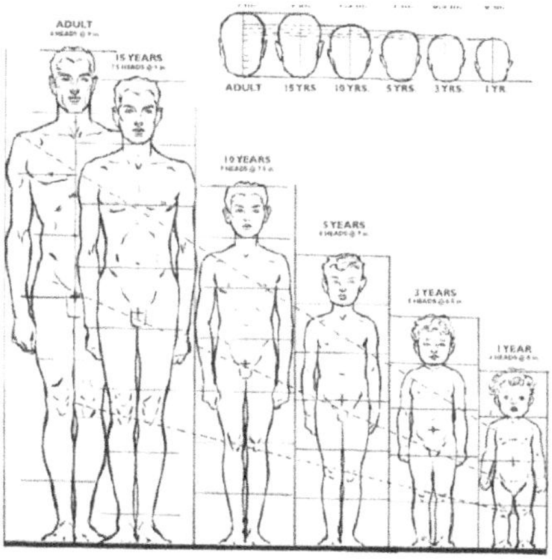

Key Signs:

-Smaller than adult, larger than a child

-Seen later in the day, often night

-Uses smoke/vape devices

-Uses cellular device

-Wears a jacket/hoodie after

What to Expect

If you have found yourself in a hot tub with any of these members, be sure to check your charts to distinguish them! So you can begin figuring out what to do now

The Elder

This specific member can be easy to tell whether or not they are in this category. The hard part is deciding whether or not you should remain silent, communicate, assert dominance, or even flee.

Considering that you were in the hot tub first and an elder approaches your party. The trick is to remain calm and welcome the uninvited guest in. With these specific members you must treat them as your own. After welcoming in the elder, you can resume your satisfying hot tub experience.

Elders are never out late and are typically seen during the day time. If anyone is to invade your hot tub, you better hope it is an elder.

Elders will typically remain silent after they receive a greeting. They are the perfect unexpected guest to accompany you and your party in your hot tub journey. The saying goes "If you don't bother them, they won't bother you".

If you are attempting to invade a party occupying the hot tub, the elders are perfect for this invasion. They typically will not mind another party joining in on the fun.

The Female

This specific member can be tricky to read. First thing you need to do when encountering a female is scanning for party members. You would be surprised to hear that they are actually quite dominant in groups. These members in groups can make you feel out of place and possibly embarrassed of yourself. The light chatter and quick glances towards your party can make you feel uneasy but fear not, doing the same back to them awards you and your party a small victory. They will begin to overthink this whole situation. They will begin to feel out of place and within 10-12 minutes you will have a hot tub to yourselves.

A single female is a neutral contender. It is an easy invasion and in most cases a single female will never enter an occupied hot tub. Dominance lacks in singular females when it comes to the spa.

Invading in on a 5+ all female party can be difficult. You will need to approach using the loud and proud method along with the barge in. Barging in on a party of females will grant absolute silence and you will be free to join in on their session.

This will only work if you outnumber their party

The Male

This type of member is often seen. These people will stick to their time frames. These people are often harmless but they are fronted with an extremely dominant look. Not to be confused with the teen, males can easily pass as one. The

difference between a teen(male) and a male is what makes it less awkward. Singular males will allow you to infiltrate them and they will greet your party upon invasion.
The risk comes when there is a group of males. Groups of males of two or more can be quite the challenge. But if this book has taught you anything, it is that anything is possible when it comes to the hot tub. The loud and proud method works best if paired with the barge in. The barge along with the male's greeting will make you and your party feel welcomed.

This will only work if you outnumber their party

The Adult

Adults occupying the hot tub is one of the worst things imaginable when it comes to finding a vacant hot tub. Invading an adult party can be harsh and not fun at first. Once you finish and have succeeded, it will all have been worth it. Adults come in two variants, Male/Female. Either of these or the combination of the two is typically a sign to not enter the hot tub. If your party is feeling risky, you can use the loud and proud method along with the barge in. It works every single time.

If you are being invaded by a party of adults, it is best to remain calm and practice the rebuttal tactic. If you don't remember, the rebuttal tactic is the reverse loud and proud. In this situation, dominance is granted to the hot tub user by default. Using this tactic along with the default dominance will ensure that you govern this spa.

*_This will only work if you outnumber their party_*

The Parent

These members have children but may not be accompanied by them.

If they are accompanied by children, this is the sign to enter that hot tub. While they are forced to look after their child, you are attempting an unexpected barge in. This method will work extremely well for yourself and your party.

The loud and proud method isn't necessarily the best option here. The issue with this tactic being used on parents, will grant absolute silence but not for the good reasons. Silence in this situation typically means you are disrupting their excursion. When entering the tub area, you may be confronted with slight anger. *A scolding* may occur if you were too loud. These scoldings are rare but aren't out of the question. After a scolding it may be awkward for the remaining duration of your hot tub experience.

The Child

Children are the easiest to invade, as they have no dominance when it comes to the hot tub. The only reason there would be to not invade with ease is that they are accompanied by a parent. A guardian and or a parent can ruin this invasion. This parent is the roadblock to your hot tub seize. In this case you would need to stick to a respectful barge in with a slight loud and proud.

Children can be annoying if left alone. These children assume they are dominant in these positions. The arrogant attitude displayed by these children will impact your hot tub experience. So always think “Is it worth it?” Checking the fallback charts would be an excellent option here.

The Teen

Teens are single handedly the worst when it comes to the hot tub. That is because you never know what you are going to get. Teens can abuse the hot tub just as easily as they can torment your party. Like usual, you will need to do the loud and proud along with the barge in method. In most cases this is a sign that you shouldn’t be going to this hot tub. It is typically best not to disturb parties of teens. These tactics will work but now you and your party will have to suffer 5-10 minutes of an awkward situation. Awkward situations when it comes to teens are horrible. Dirty looks will be exchanged between the parties and absolute silence is typically seen here.

It is just best to leave the teens alone and scan your fallback charts for other hot tubs in your area. The last thing you want for you and your party is an unpleasant hot tub experience.

The Fat Batch

Every so often you will encounter a fat hot tub member. This isn’t a bad thing! As long as this fat person is within your party. Fat tubbers are typically seen with either a shirt on to hide their gigantic and enormous stomachs or they just let it hang loose.

The way to treat these rare encounters is by treating them like regular people. Even though you might feel disgusted by these members, there is nothing to fear.
If you are worried and or have a problem with this type of person, here is how to tell the difference between them and a so-called "*regular*".

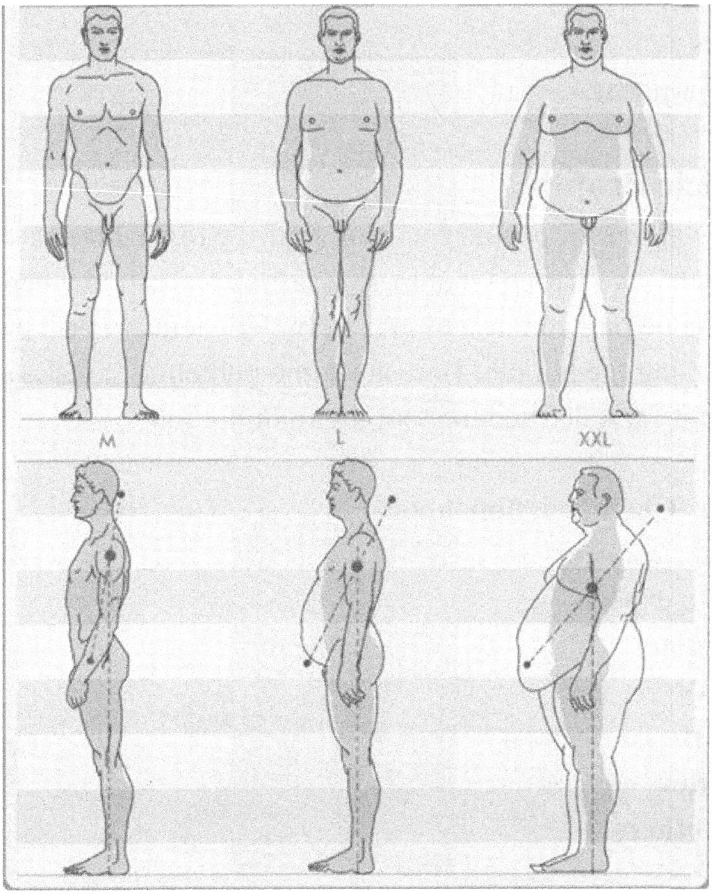

Key Signs:

-The body circumference is substantially larger

-Wider stature

-Unpleasing sight

-Thick

Bonus Members
-Hairy
-Sick
-Deformed
-Little person(Midget)
-Homeless
-Liars
-Non aquatics

Vehicle Profiling

As we all know, people can walk or drive to the hot tub. In chapter 1, we learned that there is a tricky situation where a car can be parked close to the spa but not actually be occupying the hot tub. Here are some guidelines to take an account for when scoping out the right hot tub.

Upper Class Neighborhood

Cars to expect-
-Cadillac
-BMW
-AUDI
-Bentley
-and others

Typically if you are in an upper class neighborhood, you should be seeing cars like so. If you arrive at the hot tub and parked outside of the pool gate is a janky old Nissan, then more than likely this car isn't from around here and they are occupying the hot tub.

If you are in a debate whether a car is at home or at the hot tub, then stick to that method explained above and you should be okay.

Middle Class Neighborhood
With this neighborhood it gets quite confusing. You can almost never tell if the car is here for the hot tub or for residential purposes. You just would have to use your trusty ol' Arrival, Listen, Peek method.

Lower Class Neighborhood
With this neighborhood, typically this meant you searched around your entire city for a vacant spa and couldn't find one. With these types of neighborhoods, you will never find nice cars. People in these neighborhoods also walk to their hot tub. They don't drive whatsoever. They wouldn't spare a penny towards gas in this scenario.

Chapter 5: Future Plans

In this chapter

Timesheets

Intervals

Planning ahead

There is always that one time you feel like going to the hot tub with friends. The next time you go to a hot tub before entering, you need to realize this. If you plan on coming back again, you should stick to this routine here.

Before entering the pool area, look around and perhaps take photographs of the cars parked around the area. Doing this will only help for potential hot tub experiences. After doing so, you should check your watches. Checking the time will help you further plan another hot tub session. While bathing in the tub with your friends, continue to check the time every so often. Checking the time frequently will allow you to know if people stick to their spa routines.

4:00		11:00		18:00 (6:00)	
4:15		11:15		18:15	
4:30		11:30		18:30	
4:45		11:45		18:45	
5:00		Noon		19:00 (7:00)	
5:15		12:15		19:15	
5:30		12:30		19:30	
5:45		12:45		19:45	
6:00		13:00 (1:00)		20:00 (8:00)	
6:15		13:15		20:15	
6:30		13:30		20:30	
6:45		13:45		20:45	
7:00		14:00 (2:00)		21:00 (9:00)	
7:15		14:15		21:15	
7:30		14:30		21:30	
7:45		14:45		21:45	
8:00		15:00 (3:00)		22:00 (10:00)	
8:15		15:15		22:15	
8:30		15:30		22:30	
8:45		15:45		22:45	
9:00		16:00 (4:00)		23:00 (11:00)	
9:15		16:15		23:15	
9:30		16:30		23:30	
9:45		16:45		23:45	
10:00		17:00 (5:00)		24:00 (Midnight)	
10:15		17:15		24:15	
10:30		17:30		24:30	
10:45		17:45		24:45	

Research shows us that people tend to arrive at hot tubs at even times. In this case we are talking about example: Here we have a timesheet that shows us 15 minute intervals. Hot tub members arrive at these given times. It is only on the rarest of occasions where a member will show up at a time different from these.

After having your hot tub adventure, leave the area taking more photographs along with checking the time. Doing so will help map out future experiences.

Keep record of these instances in the back of the book!

Everyone wants their hot tub experience to be pleasant so with preparing ahead of time, you will land yourself a vacant hot tub for you and your party.

Chapter 6: Gear

In this chapter

Attire

Presentation

Appeal

Necessities

Gear is extremely important when heading on down to the hot tub. In the last chapter we explained preparation. Here are some more preparation enhancements to your routine.

Typical hot tubbers will wear their sandals, bring a towel and perhaps a little bag. This is a rookie move here!

Here is what you need to bring to enhance your hot tub experience.

-Digital/disposable camera
This type of camera is perfect for quick capture and reliving your hot tub memories. The main purpose of this camera is to take pictures of the surrounding vehicles and to help enlighten future experiences.

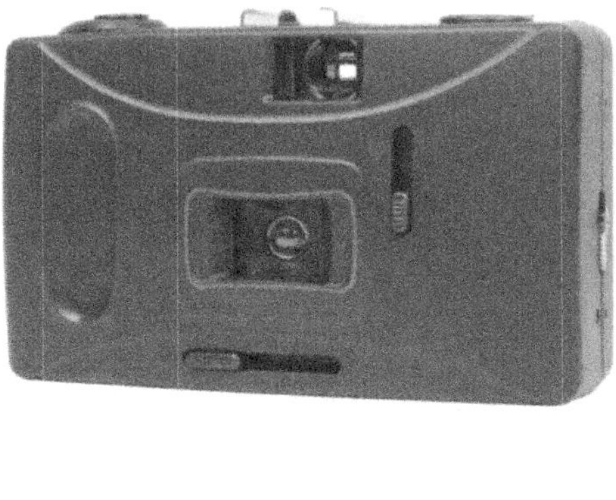

-Shoes

You may be asking why not sandals or slides? Shoes are the better option in most cases. If you and your friends decide to go hiking after or do anything that involves cardio, you will have wished you brought your shoes.

-Post hoodie

The post hoodie to be used for warming up after a pleasant session. Without bringing this, you might find yourself cool for the remainder of the drive home.

-Watch

A necessity when it comes to logging your hot tub information. If you don't have the time to log your information you may as well never attend a hot tub again.

-Toilet Paper

If you are not a resident of your hot tub, then you may be looking at unavailable restrooms. Hot tub members who need to defecate will be stranded in the hot tub. If all else fails then you will have to defecate in the surrounding bushes, causing fumes that reek of feces to wreak havoc upon your party. Toilet paper won't solve that inconvenience, but it will make sure you don't have to clean your behind in the hot tub.

-Change of clothes
A change of clothes is always a great addition to bring to your festivities. Being soaking wet and changing into a separate attire is the best option while going to the hot tub. People don't seem to understand the importance of remembering a change of clothes.

Winter and Summer
Gear remains the exact same year round. Although winter is a lot cooler, the hoodie is still preferred in the community. Wind can blow or there can be a breeze of any kind lingering around your hot tub. No matter the temperature at night, a hoodie is always a handy safety net.

Attire
When attending the hot tub there is a hidden set of guidelines that must be followed. Arriving in swim trunks or board shorts is ideal. Wearing a hoodie or shirt is an acceptable choice of wardrobe as well. The key with attire is to present yourself in the best way possible. You never know who you are going to encounter.

Presentation
Representation and presentation is always looked over in the hot tub. You need to be able to present yourself in ways where you can show everyone your true colors. Arriving in false gear can give you bad rap. The last thing people want at the hot tub is to be tricked.

Chapter 7: Scenario

In this chapter

Worst case scenario

Foot and a half rule

The hot tub is a place people come to for relaxation and sanction. Everyone in the hot tub wants to have their peaceful and pleasant time. If this book has taught you anything, it's that the hot tub is full of possibilities. Here is a list of scenarios to take into consideration while planning out your next hot tub gathering.

The Scenarios

These uncommon events must be taken into account before visiting a hot tub. Forgetting any of these intense situations will put you and your party at many disadvantages.

Failure to plan ahead leads to all sorts of potential mistakes. Professional hot tubbing is a lifestyle so when tampered with, people are left with thrown off scheduling. Scheduling is one of the most important pieces to a successful hot tub session.

With scheduling comes planning for these scenarios. You don't want to be caught off guard when entering the hot tub. Last second changes in your plan can be beneficial if scheduled in advance.

One of the worst things about hot tubbing is last second changes or unexpected events. Do your part and save your party the hassle and plan ahead!

Revolution (360 degrees)

In this situation you do not enter in any circumstance. Entering this tub is beyond an option. The only place you would be able to reside is in the direct center. We like to call that *the main focal.* Engaging in such actions is something no one should ever endure. Danger awaits in the center of the circle. There is only one time, sitting in the center of the circle is ever acceptable. That operation is known as *the desperate remedy.*

The Unconventional Arrangement

In this scenario we are given an oddly designed hot tub. In this case the seating arrangement must be mapped out prior. Not planning ahead for this style of a hot tub would be unwise. Notice the *foot and half rule* throughout the hot tub. Nearly every given point in the image, we see members distanced a foot and a half apart from one another. This rule is only used when multiple parties engage in a *collaboration.* Failure to follow this arrangement may lead to awkward situations.

The Family Affair

Members of the hot tubs will come in parties or groups of people. This specific situation shows us a family in a hot tub. The issue with this is the uneasy look on each face. When dominance is achieved early on without effort especially to a family, we receive for what's called *identical sides.* The family will scatter onto one side of the tub. While your party will remain identical on the opposing side.

Separating the members of the pack can be a poor decision when hot tubbing. Families in the hot tub tend to become protective over one another. Cornering in a circular hot tub is near impossible so everyone gets off easy in this situation.

Foot and a Half Rule(exemption)

The foot and a half rule is in your basic rule book when it comes to the hot tub. Typically the foot and a half rule applies to all tub members. There is one exception which eliminates the foot and a half rule in the hot tub. This is known as *the party shift.* As new parties begin to invade your tub time, the foot and a half rule will abolish. Even though the foot and a half rule still stands for opposing party members. The members within each party are pardoned from the foot and a half rule.

Worst Case Scenario

In the most severe cases you will find a full tub or just as you thought you found yourself a vacant tub until further realization comes and it isn't heated. The top three worst case scenarios are your biggest fears when arriving at the hot tub.

Number 1: Full Tub

In a full tub we get a cross between the 360 revolution that entitles a foot and a half rule violation and the desperate remedy spot is taken. The main focal exists within this tub experience and there is not one spot in the hot tub.

Full tubs leave a reminiscence of salt and urine. The way you can tell is by tasting the filthy concoction.

Number 2: Ice Bath

In an ice bath scenario you stumble across a deserted hot tub. Not a person in sight and all hopes are high at this point. When you and your party enter what seems to be the perfect hot tub, you all realize that the hot tub is cold. The worst part about this is all the hopes crushed in a singular moment.

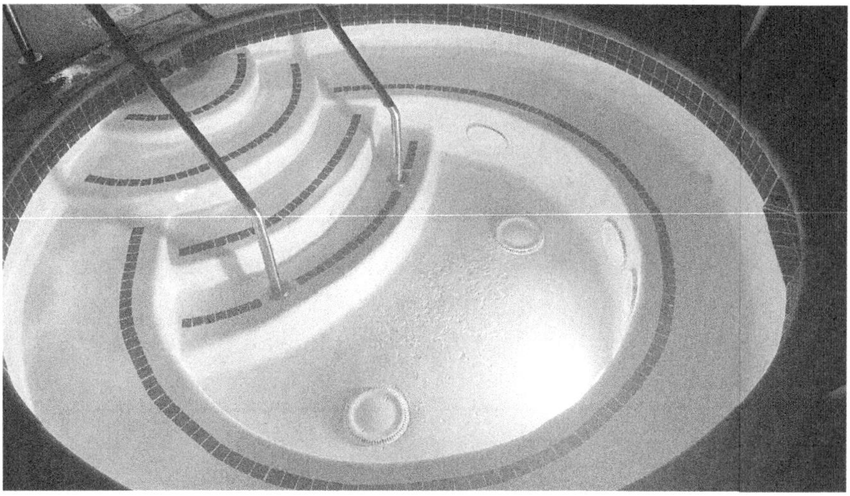

In this image you can clearly see the chilled hot tub. No sign of steam anywhere, in this case this hot tub is no good.

The cold hot tub is an ego destroyer and a faith breaker. After encountering this horrid event, individuals tend to question their life choices. Adult members of the hot tub while experiencing this scenario will notice mid life crisis symptoms.

Number 3: Defecation Keeper

In this ratchet situation, the only option you have is to leave. Lingering around the site too long can make you out to be the culprit. Attempting a full cleanse will not only take a long time, it will be near impossible. The contamination of the hot tub will entitle *a full drainage*. The refill alone will take up to an hour. Salvaging this hot tub is a waste as sad as it is to witness this occasion. This scenario can happen prior to your hot tub event. One of your members could be an official culprit. Although it is of the slightest chance of this happening it is always a possibility.

This feces filled hot tub is beyond disgusting. While it may be amusing for a short while, polluted fumes will be quick to change your mind.

These three scenarios are unexpected when hot tubbing, so be sure to remember these worst cases while scheduling your next visit.

Chapter 8: The Plan/Execution

In this chapter

Decision Making

Comfort Zone

Surroundings

Acquaintances

Encountering people at the hot tub is just such a horrendous turn of events for you and your party. A cold hot tub as well could send someone over the edge. Scheduling this perfect hot tub experience is simple if you know what you are doing… lucky for you, you own "Hot Tub Etiquette" the complete guide!

Step by Step hot tub experience

Like all events, it starts with the planning

Plan

Ask yourself, who's coming? Who's driving? What hot tub? What time?

These questions should assist your plan for your perfect hot tub experience.

Once you brainstormed the answers to these select questions, it's time to make the calls. Advancing into this section of planning can be rough, especially for the *initiator.* Attempting to get everyone on the same page is just foul. Make your calls to your exclusive guests. Once you get people on board, shoot out a text to your group chat. Ideally it is best to name the group chat "Hot Tub" so you don't get confused or mix it up with anything. This group text should include a possible time and tub location. This is only the beginning so you don't need to include all of the details.

You might find yourself in a predicament or two. In many instances, many members cannot attend the hot tub at similar hours. In this case you will need to play a little game of "*would you rather*". This game will allow you to select your crew. You will have to read between the lines and determine who is coming with you on your hot tub adventure. You need to check out the times for what works best for you. One of your guests may say 7:30 works better for them… but it might not work for you. In this case you can shoot them a text off to the side and ask why or you can tell them they aren't going. The choice is up to the initiator. It can be intimidating telling guests this heartbreaking news but this is the hot tub. There is no time for malfeasance while planning this experience.

Now that you have your select group of guests, you will need to coordinate a driving arrangement. One can drive all or you can all take separate vehicles. Keep in mind if someone needs a ride, you don't have to include them. Feel free to tell them they aren't coming.

You have your crew and you have your time. It is time to head on over to the hot tub, but first you need to schedule an arrival.

Schedule

Scheduling an arrival sounds like a huge pain. It is nothing like that at all. While driving to the hot tub, coordinate with your party if you all should just drive on up to the pool. The other option would be to slowly approach and wait. It is as simple as that.

Key Decision Making

Once you all have arrived at the hot tub, it is time to make a few decisions. Here is what to do once you have made it to the hot tub.

You and your party need to scan the road. Questions to take into consideration, Are there cars out front? Are there people heading in/out? Once you have discovered no vehicles in front of the hot tub it is time to take it to the next step.

This step requires a member or two to exit the vehicles and listen. You are listening for *the big three.* Splashing, chatter, and jets are the three sounds to listen for. These are all indications that the hot tub could be occupied. Once you and your party have concluded that none of the sounds are present it is time to journey to the next step.

This step will require *a peeker.* This member of your party must abandon the parked vehicles and make way for the hot tub area. This task asks for your peeker to find and accompany a peek hole. Finding a peek hole may be challenging but it will be worth it. Once your peeker has found a peek hole, they must examine the hot tub premises. If the coast is clear and no opposing parties are present you will officially have *the green light*. Once you have the green light, your peeker must make a choice. They can either signal the *convoy* or they can alert them by receding back to the rest of the party. Either option works great and will seal your hot tub experience.

Finally once your party has entered the gates of the hot tub, it is time to place your items into individual piles. Once you have completed this step you will have earned the right to submerge.

Just before you enter this hot tub, there is one key thing to take into account. The cold tub isn't an uncommon event. Dipping a foot or a hand into the water first can save you from poor acclimation. Your ability to acclimate quickly is stripped from you when heading into a non heated hot tub. After a light submersion, you are now ready for a full body submersion.

Familiarity and Comfort Zone

Getting used to your hot tub while bathing within it is always fun to experience. The best way to become familiar with your hot tub would consist of the following

-taking a quick scope of your surroundings

Acknowledging your surroundings is a great way to become familiar with your hot tub. Seeing where the jets can be beneficial to you and your party. Taking advantage of your surroundings can be key when with smaller parties. Knowing where the jets are can impress a special someone in your life. This little tip allows you to have an advantage over lets say another male in the picture.

-get to know the tub

When enjoying your hot tub experience, often ponder about what another member may be seeing through their own eyes. Using this trick will allow you to feel one with the hot tub.

Stepping in another's shoes is the best way to become familiar with the tub. Doing this can be extremely beneficial for future hot tubbing. In some cases you may receive double pleasure because you might drift off and imagine what another tub goer is feeling.

Feel the water and embrace the heat. You are soaking in a warm body of water that is relieving you of any sort of stress. This experience is supposed to be stress free. Find your buoyancy point and express your love for the tub. You will find yourself a lot closer to the tub than you were before.

Let the jets massage you all over your body. This is supposed to connect you to the tub. Allowing your body to feel this close to the tub will only benefit you further in your hot tub experiences.

-Acquaintance comfortability

More than likely your opposing parties within the hot tub are going to be uncomfortable. They are going to pray that you leave. They are hoping you have an ill family back home you need to care for. The bottom line is that they want you gone.

To become familiar with the other members of the hot tub, you need to examine each and every member. Doing this will make your tubbing experience more enjoyable. Staring at these other parties will allow you to access information in regards to their personal tub experiences.

Chapter 9: Tips and Tricks

In this chapter

Tactics

Operations

Hacks

Phrases

Methods

Fleeing

Luring

As we know, the possibilities are endless when it comes to the hot tub and jacuzzis. There are also plenty of tips and life hacks involving the hot tub. These are the tips and tricks for your next hot tub experience.

"I forgot my key"(key doesn't work) trick

In this devious operation your situation should consist of the following
-No key
-Person(s) occupying hot tub
-Desperate for hot tub
With this situation, you need to be willing to lie to strangers and or acquaintances. This operation relies heavily on the strangers gullibility. When arriving at the hot tub and you and your party were preparing to hop the gate you noticed the hot tub was occupied. You check your fallback charts and you realize this is the last option for hot tubs. Every other hot tub was full or not heated. When approaching the fence you need to stick to this script
lead protagonist approaches fence
***side protagonist says* "Do you have the key"**
***lead protagonist says* "Yes of course I do!"**

At this point, the stranger(s) acknowledges your existence and they will either pretend to ignore you or they will offer help. If assistance is not available yet you must initiate full engagement.
***lead protagonist beings to panic and says* "Why isn't it working?"**
***side protagonist says* "Let me help you"**

lead protagonist looks over into hot tub are and says
"Hey, can you guys help us?"

At this moment the hot tub members must get out of the hot tub and open the door for you. The success rate of this tactic is 97/100.

Phrases to ease your approach

"Lets hit her"
Often used after concluding the hot tub is vacant. This enables a singular member to alert their convoy. This phrase is perfect for shortening your sentences while keeping yourself anonymous to possible *lurkers*.

"She's full"
This terminology is often associated with occupied hot tubs. When this is said aloud, the convoy's job is to flee the area as soon as possible. Lingering around awhile after these two words have been said can result in improper hot tub etiquette.

“There’s one too many cars out here”

This is typically said on two separate occasions. The first situation is on arrival. While arriving at the hot tub a member will notice the street is flooded with vehicles. In this case a member will shout this message to the rest of the party. The second situation is while occupying a hot tub a member will exit the hot tub to scan the perimeters. The member may notice that there are several cars lurking outside of the gates. For this instance, the member will alert the rest of the party and engage in a “full loud and proud rebuttal”.

Lone survivor

This trick will only work if alone and no other parties are in the hot tub yet.

If ever headed to the hot tub alone and it meets all specifications and requirements to one's preference then this tip might save your perfect experience.

While in the hot tub you should sit in the direct center of the circle. You will be the main focal in this instance. In this situation you will assert public dominance. The good thing about this is that no one will enter your hot tub. The success rate of this operation is 75/100.

The steal and replicate

Theft is never the right thing to do. In the hot tub community we have a way of bypassing theft and passing it off as a communion loan. If a key from a resident tub member is left behind, don't be afraid to steal it. Take your new key and make copies of it. Making these copies will make it far easier for distribution. Distributing these keys to other friends will only make everyone's experience better. Always be sure to make an extra key for yourself. Once finished with the original key go ahead and leave it right where you found it. The original owner will be sure to find it.

Wind acclimation

The slight breeze or gust of wind down at the hot tub can be horrendous at given times. The last thing you want is to be unprepared for these gusts. While driving down to the hot tub it is always best to have the air conditioning on. Allow your body to get used to crispy cold air. After conditioning your body you get to enjoy your beautiful hot tub time. Now when you get out, you will already have gotten a taste of the temperature.

Giving way to the crowd

While approaching the hot tub, it isn't uncommon to encounter other parties. If you notice parties currently occupying the hot tub it is best to leave them alone and let them be. Check your fallback charts and go to your other possibly vacant hot tubs. You want to be able to enjoy yourselves, so don't ruin it for yourself. Let the crowded hot tub rest and seek out other *potentials.*

Fleeing the tub

You will notice that in many instances you will need to flee whether it is all of a sudden or it has been prolonged.

Short notice

If you need to flee and haven't had a fair warning then you must communicate with other members that you have been quite busy recently. Inform them that prior to your visit, you have been hard at work. Make them think you have better things to do. After 10-15 minutes of lying, you will need to say you need to get back at it. In this case you should be free to leave, no questions.

No one in sight

Needing to flee the tub you have been alone in isn't as easy as it seems. After getting out of the hot tub, you will need to use an inverted peek hole to plot your escape. Peeking through one of these holes will allow you to know if anyone is watching. The last thing you want is knowing that someone saw you in the hot tub alone.

Half escape

Sometimes you just can’t take the heat anymore and you might want to sit out. Instead of telling people this information that makes you appear vulnerable. You can just say you are getting out early. With this you will need to dry off real slow. You need to make the others believe you are going to leave when in reality you are cooling off.

Abandoning the finished tub

After finishing your hot tub session with your party you will want to leave. Leaving prematurely will be the improper move here. If you have finished this tub session then there isn't anything wrong with leaving. If you aren’t sure if you have finished then you will need to lurk around until a decision has been made. The last thing you want happening is leaving and then quickly turning back to go in and it's occupied. The key here is to stay until you are certain you have finished.

Luring the opposers

Just like everyone else, you want the hot tub to yourself. If you have searched out every hot tub or are just too lazy to try another it might be time to use *luring*. Luring your opponents away from the hot tub area can be hard at times. What needs to happen in this operation is a scripted plan. In advance to any hot tub sessions you should bring a football, preferably foam.

What happens next is all on you. You and your party must enter the pool area. The approach method doesn't matter. The only reason you would use this method opposed to loud and proud is if you don't have enough members. You and your party must put on enthusiastic smiles. Once completed you must cannonball, dive, and celebrate into the pool. You need to put on the false front that you are here for the pool and not the hot tub. Manipulating your opposing party is your primary goal. You need to play this off in every single way. You will have to stick to your script you practiced and rehearsed hours in advance. This can be tricky but the tip is to keep it short because the script doesn't need to be long, it needs to be believable.

Once you start passing the football around and shouting out the lines you rehearsed, you will have the rival's full attention. At this point you will need to tune out outside distractions. Sticking to the script is all you will have to do right here. Give it 10-15 minutes and the occupants will come into the pool. Your operation will have succeeded but you wil still need to remain in the pool. Getting out too soon will impose questioning with the other party. They will begin assuming it was all a gimmick. So the best thing to do is wait another 5-7 minutes and you will have your straight shot to the hot tub. The success rate of this operation is 50/100.

Chapter 10: Questions

In this chapter

Entering

Control

Frequently asked questions seem to resurface time and time again. Questions are allowed to be asked because how else would you know?

Entering tubs?

Entering hot tubs can be difficult as you may not know if it is an acceptable time to join another party.

The empty tub

This type of hot tub does not have any occupants. In this case you have the full right to enter the hot tub.

The not so full tub

This typically consists of 1-2 occupants per session. In this case it isn't admired but the choice is up to you. This is doable but not necessary.The fallback charts would be a great option here.

The party tub

With this tub specifically we are looking from 3-5 occupants per session. For this you will need to count your members and if you outnumber them, go for it. If not then the fallback charts will be the best option.

The half tub

This tub is half full and it is a combine. Different parties are in unison with this tub. The fallback charts should be your only option in this situation.

The full tub
This tub is completely full and the main focal is taken. You have no option but to leave or check your fallback charts.

What is an invasion of personal space?

Your privacy is a priority at the hot tub. There are very few instances where it is no longer a prime concern. These instances would be for these events.

-Full tub
-360 degree revolution
-Children are present
-Fats are present

When you are placed in these conditions your personal space zone shrinks dramatically. It is best to not be in the hot tub when any of these occur.

Taking control?

Getting down to the nitty gritty of hot tub etiquette shows that you can take control of the hot tub. If you have correctly followed every step and took account of every scenario then you have succeeded in taking control of the hot tub. Studying this guide book can show you the keys that allow you to take control. Dominance, whether its public or discrete, is the most important concept in regards to the hot tub.

Location, times, spots?

Usually it comes down to your location and the popularity of the hot tub when you need to find one. Lucky for you this book teaches you the ways around occupied hot tubs regardless of popularity.

Best spots in the hot tub to sit

The best spot to sit in the hot tub is the opposing side of the steps. This spot is the most superior place in a hot tub if people are already in the hot tub. Sitting in this spot shows to everyone else that you are the direct host of this hot tub session. What you say goes in this scenario. When people enter the hot tub they feel as if they need to ask for permission to enter. You may receive a head bow or a nod of respect when members enter. You leave other members with one of two options, each granting you full respect. They acknowledge your position of authority and they physically show you their corporation. The second option is that they will fail to make eye contact due to the amount of intimidation they are receiving.

Best spots in the pool area(Excluding hot tub)

Sit back and relax or grab a chair. One of these options will grant you mutual respect. They know you won't attempt to seize authority. You will also know they mean no harm. It is the perfect spot while hanging around the pool area. Linger around the hot tub so you can get your place in line in case friends show up later.

Best times to go to the hot tub

Check out your interval timesheets for this information. If you haven't filled out your sheets yet then the best time to go on down to the hot tub is after 9 PM. In general most parties will have fled the hot tub by then. If you encounter anyone there at this time, it will be teens. In this case, you will need to check the fallback charts and head on over to another possible vacant hot tub.

Best places to enter a hot tub you're not allowed in
The key to this segment is using the no key trick. Using this trick only works if people are residing within the pool's premises. If no one is there, you better know how to hop a fence. Hopping fences is a key ability when recreationally hot tubbing. In most cases this will be the only way in. Depending on the type of lock you can pick your way in. In some cases you can use a credit card to enter the pool area. It takes some practice but once you get the hang of it, it is handy.

Appendix

Interval time sheets

TIME	ACTIVITY		TIME	ACTIVITY	
6:00			2:00		
6:15			2:15		
6:30			2:30		
6:45			2:45		
7:00			3:00		
7:15			3:15		
7:30			3:30		
7:45			3:45		
8:00			4:00		
8:15			4:15		
8:30			4:30		
8:45			4:45		
9:00			5:00		
9:15			5:15		
9:30			5:30		
9:45			5:45		
10:00			6:00		
10:15			6:15		
10:30			6:30		
10:45			6:45		
11:00			7:00		
11:15			7:15		
11:30			7:30		
11:45			7:45		
12:00			8:00		
12:15			8:15		
12:30			8:30		
12:45			8:45		
1:00			9:00		
1:15			9:15		
1:30			9:30		
1:45			9:45		

Interval time sheets

TIME	ACTIVITY		TIME	ACTIVITY	
6:00			2:00		
6:15			2:15		
6:30			2:30		
6:45			2:45		
7:00			3:00		
7:15			3:15		
7:30			3:30		
7:45			3:45		
8:00			4:00		
8:15			4:15		
8:30			4:30		
8:45			4:45		
9:00			5:00		
9:15			5:15		
9:30			5:30		
9:45			5:45		
10:00			6:00		
10:15			6:15		
10:30			6:30		
10:45			6:45		
11:00			7:00		
11:15			7:15		
11:30			7:30		
11:45			7:45		
12:00			8:00		
12:15			8:15		
12:30			8:30		
12:45			8:45		
1:00			9:00		
1:15			9:15		
1:30			9:30		
1:45			9:45		

Interval time sheets

TIME	ACTIVITY		TIME	ACTIVITY	
6:00			2:00		
6:15			2:15		
6:30			2:30		
6:45			2:45		
7:00			3:00		
7:15			3:15		
7:30			3:30		
7:45			3:45		
8:00			4:00		
8:15			4:15		
8:30			4:30		
8:45			4:45		
9:00			5:00		
9:15			5:15		
9:30			5:30		
9:45			5:45		
10:00			6:00		
10:15			6:15		
10:30			6:30		
10:45			6:45		
11:00			7:00		
11:15			7:15		
11:30			7:30		
11:45			7:45		
12:00			8:00		
12:15			8:15		
12:30			8:30		
12:45			8:45		
1:00			9:00		
1:15			9:15		
1:30			9:30		
1:45			9:45		

A letter from our field researcher

"Dear colleagues,

I have some very very interesting experiences at my hot tub right here in Moorpark, California. I personally am getting to the point where I am going to have to start emailing the HOA of this community pool for them to get their act in order. I have been going to this hot tub for the last 5 years. I am not a current resident of the Highlands community in Moorpark but I can use that pool whenever I want to. I have my own key, I have a gate code and no "official resident" is going to stop me from staying warm with my good friends.

I would like to talk about my main friends I attend this hot tub with. We will talk about them later.

There are actually two different hot tubs we like to call them, "The Right Tub and The Left Tub." We don't go to the right tub as much anymore because the tub and the pool aren't heated as often anymore, and when the tub is heated over there you can barely stand it because they turn the temperature to 110 degrees.

We are left side tub hitters 99.9% of the time. If both the right and left tubs are occupied up at the Highlands community then there is a chance we will just go hit the Mountain Meadows tub but we don't like to go there often because she is a big downgrade. Musty fumes along with the sight of underwater fecal matter isn't the best place to soak in.

Sincerely,

Nathaniel Cheddar

(Field Researcher)"

The Hot Tub Dictionary

"Is it worth it?"
The value scale of the hot tub
EX. "Is it worth it if there are that many people here?"

Approach
You're tactic of invading a hot tub
EX. "How should we approach this time?"

Peek hole
Holes within a hot tubs premises that allow you to examine the hot tub
EX. "Look through that peek hole to see if anyones there!"

Silent approach
The quiet discrete choice of approach to invade a hot tub
EX. "Let's go with the silent approach, it's only us"

Loud and proud approach
The obnoxious choice of approach to invade a hot tub
EX. "Let's go with the loud and proud approach, we got everyone here!"

Absolute silence
The level of noise measured by units of voice and splashes
EX. "We have achieved absolute silence, it's time to go in"

Awkward situation
A situation in which no one speaks
EX. "We had an awkward situation back there!"

The Hot Tub Dictionary

Last straggler
A singular member that wants to leave due to invasion but is embarrassed due to enforcement
EX. "Look at that last straggler, he should just leave"

Trunks
A piece of swim gear for your lower half
EX. "Look at him taking off his trunks!"

After hours
Anytime past 10 PM
EX. "These people are still here even in after hours"

A Scolding
A singular member confronts another tub goer
EX. "Remember when you received a scolding last week"

A regular
A tub member who appears frequently
EX. "She's a regular, she is here almost everytime we come"

The main focal
A spot in the hot tub where everyone's main focus is on you
EX. "Looks like im the main focal today"

The desperate remedy
An occasion where its an acceptable time to be the main focal
EX. "I think i need the desperate remedy"

The Hot Tub Dictionary

Foot and a half rule
The rule that lays out the distance between each member
EX. "He isn't obeying the foot and a half rule!"

Collaboration
When multiple parties engage in a hot tub session
EX. "We can't go here, there's a collaboration"

Identical sides
An event in which two parties divide onto opposite sides
EX. "Looks like we got an identical sides situation here"

The party shift
When more people invade the tub, 3 ½ rule is abolished
EX. "The party shift was brutal today"

A full drainage
When a hot tub needs to be drained due to defecation
EX. "We encountered a full drainage the other day"

Initiator
The person who created the plans to a hot tub session
EX. "Ralph is an asshole, who let him be the initiator?"

Would you rather
The event in which the initiator chooses a person over another
EX. "Would you rather have Ralph or Steven because Steven can't make it til 7?"

The Hot Tub Dictionary

The big three
The signs of splashing, chatter and jets
EX. “The big three were present at that hot tub”

A peeker
A member whose task is to use a peek hole
EX. “You are a peeker today! No questions”

The green light
The indication that the hot tub is ready to be used
EX. “We got a green light!”

Convoy
Cars of parties parked outside of the pool’s premises
EX. “We got a convoy outside boys!”

Lurkers
Potential hot tub users
EX. “We got a couple lurkers outside”

Potentials
Potential hot tubs that can be used
EX. “this one’s full, let's check other potentials”

Luring
The act of leading a tub member away from the hot tub
EX. “

Pool area

The area around the hot tub but within the gates of the pool

EX. "People are in the pool area but not the hot tub"

Records
(Courtesy of field researcher Nathaniel Cheddar)

4/13/2019

TIME	ACTIVITY	TIME	ACTIVITY
6:00		2:00	
6:15		2:15	
6:30		2:30	
6:45		2:45	
7:00		3:00	
7:15		3:15	
7:30		3:30	
7:45		3:45	
8:00		4:00	
8:15		4:15	
8:30		4:30	
8:45		4:45	
9:00		5:00	
9:15		5:15	
9:30		5:30	
9:45		5:45	
10:00		6:00	No one
10:15		6:15	No one Again
10:30		6:30	Convoy outside
10:45		6:45	Convoy leaves
11:00		7:00	1 party enters
11:15		7:15	They don't come into hot tub
11:30		7:30	Teen Approached
11:45		7:45	Nobody
12:00		8:00	Two tubbers invade
12:15		8:15	Still here
12:30		8:30	Both fled
12:45		8:45	Party attempts loud And proud
1:00		9:00	I rebuttal loud And proud
1:15		9:15	They flee
1:30		9:30	Nobody
1:45		9:45	Nothing

Records cont.

4/13/2020

TIME	ACTIVITY		TIME	ACTIVITY	
6:00			2:00		
6:15			2:15		
6:30			2:30		
6:45			2:45		
7:00			3:00		
7:15			3:15		
7:30			3:30		
7:45			3:45		
8:00			4:00		
8:15			4:15		
8:30			4:30		
8:45			4:45		
9:00			5:00		
9:15	Nothing		5:15		
9:30	No one Again		5:30		
9:45	No one		5:45		
10:00			6:00	Teen Approached	
10:15			6:15	They don't come into hot tub	
10:30			6:30		
10:45			6:45		
11:00			7:00		
11:15	Nobody		7:15		
11:30	Nobody		7:30		
11:45			7:45	1 party enters	
12:00			8:00	Still here	
12:15			8:15	They flee	
12:30			8:30		
12:45			8:45		
1:00			9:00		
1:15			9:15		
1:30			9:30		
1:45			9:45		

Records cont.

4/13/2021

TIME	ACTIVITY		TIME	ACTIVITY	
6:00			2:00		
6:15			2:15		
6:30			2:30		
6:45			2:45	No one	
7:00			3:00	No one Again	
7:15			3:15	Nobody	
7:30			3:30	Nobody	
7:45			3:45	Nothing	
8:00			4:00		
8:15			4:15		
8:30			4:30		
8:45			4:45		
9:00			5:00		
9:15			5:15		
9:30			5:30		
9:45			5:45		
10:00			6:00		
10:15			6:15		
10:30			6:30		
10:45			6:45		
11:00			7:00		
11:15			7:15		
11:30			7:30		
11:45			7:45		
12:00			8:00		
12:15			8:15		
12:30			8:30	1 party Arrives(silent)	
12:45			8:45	They flee	
1:00			9:00		
1:15			9:15	Teen enters hot tub	
1:30			9:30	Still here	
1:45			9:45		

Records cont.

7/4/2021

TIME	ACTIVITY	TIME	ACTIVITY
6:00	Nothing	2:00	
6:15	No one	2:15	
6:30	Nobody	2:30	
6:45	No one Again	2:45	
7:00	Nobody	3:00	
7:15		3:15	
7:30		3:30	
7:45		3:45	
8:00		4:00	
8:15		4:15	Two parties enter
8:30		4:30	Someone shits
8:45		4:45	
9:00		5:00	Pool man drains spa
9:15		5:15	I exit hot tub
9:30		5:30	
9:45		5:45	
10:00		6:00	
10:15		6:15	
10:30		6:30	
10:45		6:45	I enter hot tub
11:00		7:00	Cleaned and refilled
11:15		7:15	
11:30		7:30	
11:45		7:45	5 parties enter
12:00		8:00	360 revolution
12:15		8:15	Teen enters hot tub
12:30		8:30	Desperate remedy
12:45		8:45	Awkward situation
1:00		9:00	Jets break
1:15		9:15	A Scolding occurs
1:30		9:30	
1:45		9:45	Still here

Official Estimates for 2025
(Courtesy Nathaniel Cheddar)

Fourth of July weekend:
"That weekend will be slammed packed with all kinds of people. Expect urinated waters along with full tubs across the grid. There will be possible draining due to defecations. Trying to squeeze into one of these hot tubs will be labor intensive. Your best bet is to head on down to the hot tub early in the morning. The tubs will begin to fill at 11 AM sharp. People will be staying late so don't expect to get any tub time before 10 PM. Possible after hours sessions may be in play so if you are planning on possibly tubbing after the spa closes be sure to keep an eye out."

Labor Day weekend:
"This weekend is looking content as of right now. You should be safe to head on into the hot tubs early on in the day. Coming in around 1 PM you will notice parties entering and exiting. All of that hot tub traffic should clear up around 8 or 9 PM. Your safest bet is to go around 9:30 PM for the best hot tub experience."

Christmas Eve:
"Christmas Eve is looking rather open this upcoming year. People tend to stay inside or perform indoor activities. The hot tub will be free all day except maybe around 5 PM. At this time you might encounter a person or two. If you want to play it safe it is best to not go around 4 to 6 PM."

Halloween:

"This day will be great to head over to the hot tub. Even though the sight of children or parents occupying the hot tub will be low. You have high chances of encountering teenagers. These hostile tub members on Halloween might not be the best call. If you want to head on over for a hot tub session it will be best to finish on up before 7 PM."

Spring Break:

"This week long weekend will be a horrible time for the hot tub. You may be able to squeeze in a hot tub session here and there but it is advised to stay away for that week. The pool will be filled with all kinds of tub members. The hot tub will be occupied most of the days during the week. If you plan on going it will be best to go in the morning, finishing up by 10 AM."

Memorial Day weekend:

"This weekend won't be much fun for recreational and professional tub goers. The best days during the weekend to attend the hot tub are early Saturday and Sunday. Monday should be all cleared up after 5 PM. If you want a high risk high reward scenario head on over Friday night."

MY PERFECT HOT TUB EXPERIENCE

IS THE TUB EMPTY?	YES/NO
IS THE HOT TUB HOT?	YES/NO
IS THE TUB'S LIGHT WORKING?	YES/NO
IS THE WATER CLEAR?	YES/NO
DO THE JETS WORK?	YES/NO
IS THE TUB BIG ENOUGH?	YES/NO
HAS ANYONE TRIED COMING IN?	YES/NO
HAVE YOU IMPRESSED ANYONE?	YES/NO
ARE YOU DISPLAYING DOMINANCE?	YES/NO
IS THE VISIBILITY GOOD?	YES/NO
DO YOU HEAR VEICHLES OUTSIDE?	YES/NO
ARE YOU DOCUMENTING YOUR TIMESHEET?	YES/NO
HAVE YOU TAKEN PHOTOGRAPHS?	YES/NO
HAVE YOU BROUGHT YOUR POST HOODIE?	YES/NO
ARE YOU PRESENTING YOURSELF WELL?	YES/NO
IS THE 3 1/2 FOOT RULE BEING OBEYED?	YES/NO
HAVE YOU PLAYED OUT DIFFERENT SCENARIOS?	YES/NO
ARE YOU ALREADY PLANNING FUTURE TUBBING?	YES/NO
ARE YOU SCANNING YOUR SURROUNDINGS?	YES/NO
ARE YOU BECOMING FAMILIAR WITH THE TUB?	YES/NO
ARE YOU CHECKING YOUR WATCH?	YES/NO
ARE YOU SITTING IN THE BEST SPOT POSSIBLE?	YES/NO
ARE YOU ENJOYING YOURSELF?	YES/NO

MY PERFECT HOT TUB EXPERIENCE

IS THE TUB EMPTY?	YES/NO
IS THE HOT TUB HOT?	YES/NO
IS THE TUB'S LIGHT WORKING?	YES/NO
IS THE WATER CLEAR?	YES/NO
DO THE JETS WORK?	YES/NO
IS THE TUB BIG ENOUGH?	YES/NO
HAS ANYONE TRIED COMING IN?	YES/NO
HAVE YOU IMPRESSED ANYONE?	YES/NO
ARE YOU DISPLAYING DOMINANCE?	YES/NO
IS THE VISIBILITY GOOD?	YES/NO
DO YOU HEAR VEICHLES OUTSIDE?	YES/NO
ARE YOU DOCUMENTING YOUR TIMESHEET?	YES/NO
HAVE YOU TAKEN PHOTOGRAPHS?	YES/NO
HAVE YOU BROUGHT YOUR POST HOODIE?	YES/NO
ARE YOU PRESENTING YOURSELF WELL?	YES/NO
IS THE 3 1/2 FOOT RULE BEING OBEYED?	YES/NO
HAVE YOU PLAYED OUT DIFFERENT SCENARIOS?	YES/NO
ARE YOU ALREADY PLANNING FUTURE TUBBING?	YES/NO
ARE YOU SCANNING YOUR SURROUNDINGS?	YES/NO
ARE YOU BECOMING FAMILIAR WITH THE TUB?	YES/NO
ARE YOU CHECKING YOUR WATCH?	YES/NO
ARE YOU SITTING IN THE BEST SPOT POSSIBLE?	YES/NO
ARE YOU ENJOYING YOURSELF?	YES/NO

MY PERFECT HOT TUB EXPERIENCE

IS THE TUB EMPTY?	YES/NO
IS THE HOT TUB HOT?	YES/NO
IS THE TUB'S LIGHT WORKING?	YES/NO
IS THE WATER CLEAR?	YES/NO
DO THE JETS WORK?	YES/NO
IS THE TUB BIG ENOUGH?	YES/NO
HAS ANYONE TRIED COMING IN?	YES/NO
HAVE YOU IMPRESSED ANYONE?	YES/NO
ARE YOU DISPLAYING DOMINANCE?	YES/NO
IS THE VISIBILITY GOOD?	YES/NO
DO YOU HEAR VEICHLES OUTSIDE?	YES/NO
ARE YOU DOCUMENTING YOUR TIMESHEET?	YES/NO
HAVE YOU TAKEN PHOTOGRAPHS?	YES/NO
HAVE YOU BROUGHT YOUR POST HOODIE?	YES/NO
ARE YOU PRESENTING YOURSELF WELL?	YES/NO
IS THE 3 1/2 FOOT RULE BEING OBEYED?	YES/NO
HAVE YOU PLAYED OUT DIFFERENT SCENARIOS?	YES/NO
ARE YOU ALREADY PLANNING FUTURE TUBBING?	YES/NO
ARE YOU SCANNING YOUR SURROUNDINGS?	YES/NO
ARE YOU BECOMING FAMILIAR WITH THE TUB?	YES/NO
ARE YOU CHECKING YOUR WATCH?	YES/NO
ARE YOU SITTING IN THE BEST SPOT POSSIBLE?	YES/NO
ARE YOU ENJOYING YOURSELF?	YES/NO

Fallback Charts

EXAMPLE

Locations	**Tub 1 Address*	**Tub 2 Address*	**Tub 3 Address*		
Busiest	*8pm*	*9pm*	*7:30pm*		
Least busiest	*5pm*	*4pm*	*10pm*		

Locations					
Busiest					
Least busiest					

Locations					
Busiest					
Least busiest					

Locations					
Busiest					
Least busiest					

NOTES

NOTES

NOTES

NOTES

Made in the USA
Las Vegas, NV
17 March 2025

19693925R00059